a book of

Bliss

a book of

Bliss

thoughts to make you smile

SOURCEBOOKS, INC.®
NAPERVILLE, ILLINOIS

Published by Sourcebooks, Inc.
P.O. Box 4410, Naperville, Illinois 60567-4410
(630) 961-3900
FAX: (630) 961-2168
www.sourcebooks.com

Library of Congress Cataloging-in-Publication Data

A Book of bliss : thoughts to make you smile.
     p. cm.
  ISBN 1-57071-966-7
  1. Happiness--Quotations, maxims, etc. 2. Conduct of
life--Quotations, maxims, etc.
  PN6084.H3 B66 2002
  082--dc21

                                                    2001007262

Printed and bound in the United States of America
LB 10 9 8 7 6 5

The quiet song of every soul
creates a global symphony.

———

*Make happy those who are near,
and those who are far will come.*
—Chinese proverb

No matter how old you are, look back
on your life and recall all the good
things. You'll realize how much you
have to be thankful for.

———————

*It is never too late to be
what you might have been.*
—George Eliot

Never underestimate a friend,
for during tough times
their love proves strongest.

———————

*Be a friend to thyself,
and others will be so too.*
–Thomas Fuller

Bliss is finding that twenty-dollar bill in your jeans pocket that you'd forgotten was there.

———

There is no house like the house of belonging.
—David Whyte

Giving of yourself and not
expecting anything in return
brings joy to you and to others.

––––––––––

Mental sunshine will cause the flowers
of peace, happiness, and prosperity to
grow upon the face of the Earth.
Be a creator of mental sunshine.
—graffiti on a wall in Berkeley, California

Enjoy the sounds of nature—
they will bring you serenity.

———————

With each sunrise, we start anew.
—Anonymous

Tea is great on its own,
but it's infinitely better
when coupled with a book.

————————

Some say life is the thing,
but I prefer reading.
—Ruth Rendell

Laughter with family and friends is a
gift to yourself and to those you love.

————————

Nobody ever died of laughter.
–Max Beerbohm

 A Book of Bliss

The best thing about good friends is the way they make you feel like the best version of yourself.

_____

Laughter is the shortest distance between two people.
—Victor Borge

Be mindful of each glorious moment
and savor the wealth of goodness in
your life.

———————

*The secret of happiness is
not in doing what one likes,
but in liking what one has to do.*
—James M. Barrie

Every dark rain shower leaves behind
a chandelier of sunlit droplets.

———

Deep in their roots,
All flowers keep the light.
—Theodore Roethke

Being happy is a choice—one that is easily made and highly rewarding.

He that is of a merry heart hath a continual feast.
—Proverbs 15:15

An act of love today will flow
as a wave of peace through
the future of mankind.

———————

World peace is us….
We are each walking agents of the
vision of peace we carry inside us.
—Kathleen Vande Kieft

A baby's smile reawakens your
belief in the innocence of youth.

———————

*Youth is happy because it
has the ability to see beauty.
Anyone who keeps the ability
to see beauty never grows old.*
—Franz Kafka

A great day begins and
ends in happiness.

————

Earth's crammed with heaven.
–Elizabeth Barrett Browning

Even if you can't see it,
the sun is always shining.

———————

When you get to the end of your rope,
tie a knot and hang on.
—Anonymous

Patience is a gift you give to others
that returns to you in kind.

———————

Be content with what you have;
rejoice in the way things are.
—Lao Tzu

Embrace life's passions, but seek
lasting contentment.

---

*If you are content, you have enough to
live comfortably.*
—Plautus

Think about your favorite song.
Dream of driving down a country road
on an Indian summer day as it plays on
the radio. Now, don't you feel good?

Never be afraid to sit a while and think.
—Lorraine Hansberry

Be proud of yourself every day. There will always be a good reason.

———————

Everything that is done in the world is done by hope.
—Martin Luther

Take time to create something
and share it with others. Whether
you make a meal or paint a picture,
you will be sharing a part
of yourself.

———————

*Each day, and the living of it, has to be
a conscious creation in which discipline
and order are relieved with some play
and pure foolishness.*
—May Sarton

Carpe diem.

———————

*Why not seize pleasure at once? How
often is happiness destroyed by
preparation, foolish preparation!*
—Jane Austen

Spend an afternoon near water. Marvel at its music, presence, and adaptability.

———————

Oh, for the wonder that
bubbles into my soul.
—D. H. Lawrence

Autumn leaves and the smell of
winter coming make it even better
to sleep in on Saturday morning
under a big pile of blankets.

————————

*I like living. I have sometimes
been wildly, despairingly, acutely
miserable, racked with sorrow, but
through it all I still know quite certainly
that just to be alive is a grand thing.*
—Agatha Christie

Pay compliments as often as possible.
It will make both of you feel good.

———————

*To love another person is to
see the face of God.*
—Victor Hugo, *Les Miserables*

Plant a tree. Know that you are
responsible for that tree.
Watch it grow.

———————

*It is better to have a rich soul
than to be rich.*
—Olga Korbut

Learn something new and then
teach it to someone else. You will
both have something new and
interesting to talk about.

———————

The only true gift is a portion of thyself.
—Ralph Waldo Emerson

Be illuminated by the love
that surrounds you.

_____

The more light you allow within you, the
brighter the world you live in will be.
—Shakti Gawain

Anyone can have friends, but being a friend is an achievement.

———————

Blessed is the influence of one true, loving human soul on another.
—George Eliot

The greatest gift you can give to the world is yourself; so cherish your gift.

———————

Learn to get in touch with the silence within yourself and know that everything in this life has a purpose, there are no mistakes, no coincidences, all events are blessings given to us to learn from.
—Elizabeth Kubler-Ross

Is there any place filled with more
warmth and love than your family's
kitchen while a holiday feast
is being prepared?

———————

*Home is not where you live but
where they understand you.*
—Christian Morgenstern

Exercise your right to be joyful.

———————

Each of my days are miracles.
I won't waste my days;
I won't throw away a miracle.
—Kelley Vickstrom

The seasons please the senses differently; feel summer, smell autumn, taste winter, and see spring.

_____

The greatest of all miracles is to be alive.
—Thich Nhat Hanh

Remember that although you are one of many, you are singularly unique.

———————

Have a love affair with yourself. Until you can have a love affair with you, you can't begin to have as much fun as there is with somebody else.
—Viki King

Balance work with fun and
your heart will stay young.

———————

Have regular hours for work and play;
make each day both useful and pleasant,
and prove that you understand the
worth of time by employing it well. Then
youth will be delightful, old age will
bring few regrets, and life will become a
beautiful success, in spite of poverty.
—Louisa May Alcott, *Little Women*

Hope can be found in everything.

———————

The more I wonder…the more I love.
—Alice Walker

Your face is the canvas for your
message to others. Paint it with a smile.

———

*Giving is the highest expression
of our power.*
—Vivian Greene

If you have a favorite poem or song, learn it by heart. When you really need it, you'll always be able to recall something that gives you joy.

––––––––––

Life is ours to be spent, not to be saved.
––D.H. Lawrence

If you always keep your eyes on the path, you miss miles and miles of beautiful scenery.

———————

The great pleasure in life is doing what people say you cannot do.
—Walter Bagehot

Complimenting the good deed of another is a simple way to ensure that such deeds will be repeated.

――――――――

Never doubt that a small group of committed citizens can change the world. Indeed, it's the only thing that has.
—Margaret Mead

Nothing cures the blues like a warm
loaf of bread and a caring friend.

————————

Joy is prayer—Joy is strength—
Joy is love—Joy is a net by which
you can catch souls. She gives
most who gives with joy.
—Mother Teresa

If you've ever watched a cat lie on its back soaking up the sun, you know just how simple life's pleasures can be.

_____

Happiness to a dog is what lies on the other side of a door.
—Charlton Ogburn Jr.

To share love is to know another.

———————

Only the heart speaks to the heart.
I needed to tell you my story as I
need to hear yours, so that we may
share our secrets and trust our hearts.
—Judy Collins

Give generously of yourself and you
will have all that you need.

————————

*Kind words can be short and
easy to speak, but their echoes
are truly endless.*
—Mother Teresa

The world isn't so big that you do not
make a difference just by living your life.

———————

Whoever is happy will make
others happy too.
—Anne Frank

Even when you have nothing, you still have yourself, and that's the most important thing.

———————

You are not only good to yourself, but the cause of goodness in others.
—Socrates

You have done the right thing when you can look back and be glad you did it.

If you obey all the rules you miss all the fun.
—Katharine Hepburn

There is fun in a sea of umbrellas
on a crowded city street.

———————

*The difference between landscape
and landscape is small, but there is a
great difference in the beholders.*
—Ralph Waldo Emerson

When someone asks you for a favor,
be glad that you can do something
for someone else and let them
know that you are glad.

———————

*Remember that happiness is a way
of travel—not a destination.*
—Roy M. Goodman

Do not seek peace and you
surely will find it.

———————

*If only we'd stop trying to be happy we
could have a pretty good time.*
—Edith Wharton

Life is short. Let yourself feel bliss.

———————————

*If you haven't got all the things you
want, be grateful for the things you
don't have that you don't want.*
—Anonymous

It helps to have a healthy body if
you want a healthy spirit.

———————

Balance is beautiful.
—Mikiyo Ohno

There is one thing that you can do better than anyone else in the whole world. When you discover what it is, the world will be yours.

Doing the best at this moment puts you in the best place for the next moment.
—Oprah Winfrey

Make a list of things that make you
glad you're alive—favorite movies,
books, albums, foods, places, people—
and keep it with you to continually
update and as a reminder
of how good life can be.

———————

Come friends, the quick and the dead,
from overseas and from the cemeteries.
And if we have already managed to
gather here so nicely, let's have a feast
in the garden to beat all feasts.
—George Konrád

A Book of Bliss

Bring a shout of joy to your own
corner of the world today.

————————

*I'm convinced that it's energy
and humor. The two of them
combined equal charm.*
—Judith Krantz

Not all great thinkers are as wise
as children. Spend time getting
to know some incredible kids.

———————

*The only way to speak the
truth is to speak lovingly.*
—Henry David Thoreau

Do one unselfish thing each day and you will have lived a life of kindness.

———————

The best and most beautiful things in the world cannot be seen or even touched. They must be felt with the heart.
—Helen Keller

Out in the country, with no city lights to obscure the millions of stars in the night sky, you can see how centuries ago people saw lions, serpents, archers, and hares in the heavens.

———————

There's a reason heaven and earth
go on enduring forever:
their life isn't their own
so their life goes on forever.
—Lao Tzu

A friend is someone you may only see once every couple years, and yet every time you see him, it's as though no time has passed at all.

———————

It is one of the blessings of old friends that you can afford to be stupid with them.
—Ralph Waldo Emerson

For fun, wear something that
makes you smile today.

Happiness makes up in height
for what it lacks in length.
—Robert Frost

Don't be afraid to say what's on
your mind. You'll be surprised by how
many people are willing to listen.

———————

Celebrate what you want to see more of.
—Tom Peters

You are free. You're Superman (or woman). You are invincible.

―――――――

Choose thy love. Love thy choice.
—German proverb

It is bliss when your parents tell
you that you make them proud.
It doesn't matter how old you are,
their approval still counts in spades.

———————

*It's good to have an end to journey
toward; but it's the journey that
matters, in the end.*
—Ursula K. LeGuin

Under your window, a miniature sea of vibrant reds, yellows, violets, and blues signals the onset of spring with the flowers you planted last fall.

———————

*Imagination is the highest kite
one can fly*
—Lauren Bacall

On an early winter morning, as
you pause with shovel in hand, let the
silent white blanket that covers your
town remind you that every "curse" is a
blessing in disguise.

---

*It seems to me that we often,
almost sulkily, reject the good that
God offers us because, at the moment,
we expected some other good.*
—C.S. Lewis

Experience other cultures and learn that the world is not as big as you thought.

————————

There is no great difference in the reality of one country or another, because it is always people you meet everywhere. They may look different or be dressed differently, or may have a different education or position. But they are all the same. They are all people to be loved.
—Mother Teresa

That first kiss of spring after a long
gray winter is bliss.

———————

*I've gotten all the news I need from
the weather report. Hey, I've got
nothing to do today but smile...*
—Paul Simon

Fulfillment can be as simple as placing the last piece of a jigsaw puzzle.

————————

Success for the striver washes away the effort of striving.
—Pindar

Joy is realizing that all of nature's
beauty exists for your pleasure.

————————

Art for art's sake is an empty phrase.
Art for the sake of the true, art for the
sake of the good and the beautiful, that
is the faith I am searching for.
—George Sand

Anything that you want,
you can achieve.

_____

The future belongs to those who
believe in the beauty of their dreams.
—Anonymous

Hug your family and friends and
let them know you care.

———————

Action is the antidote to despair.
—Joan Baez

Remember being a kid and
running so fast that the wind
gave up trying to catch you?

―――――――

Shoot for the moon. Even if you miss it,
you'll land amongst the stars.
—Anonymous

A Book of Bliss

Enjoy the little things today.

———————

Happiness? That's nothing more than health and a poor memory.
—Albert Schweitzer

Temperance is wise,
but exuberance is more fun.

———————

*It is not the years in your life but the
life in your years that counts.*
—Adlai Stevenson

Watch a silly movie and have a good laugh. You'll feel a hundred times better for having done it.

———————

We are all worms, but I do believe I am a glow-worm.
—Winston Churchill

Learn to give great hugs.
It's a nice hobby.

———————

*One need not hope
in order to undertake;
nor succeed in order to persevere.*
—William the Silent

What did you wish you could be when you grew up? Take some time right now to dream that dream again.

Reach high, for stars lie hidden in your soul. Dream deep, for every dream precedes the goal.
—Pamela Vaull Starr

Consider how your love affects
everything you do and
everyone you encounter.

————————

Don't hate. It's too big a burden to bear.
—Martin Luther King

A Book of Bliss

It is respect for others that
validates your own actions.

––––––––––

One's life has value so long as one
attributes value to the life of others,
by means of love, friendship,
indignation, and compassion.
—Simone de Beauvoir

Play in the rain and laugh
about the muddiness.

———————

*The invariable mark of wisdom is to
see the miraculous in the common.*
—Ralph Waldo Emerson

Little haiku poems
May seem inconsequential,
But they'll make your day.

———————

Poetry is a way of taking life
by the throat.
—Robert Frost

It's daunting to contemplate the
human capacity for despair;
yet when you realize that it mirrors
the capacity for joy, you come
closer to understanding the beauty
of man's innate intricacies.

———————

*Knowledge of what is possible is
the beginning of happiness.*
—George Santayana

A Book of Bliss

Hold someone's hand and share
security and warmth.

---

*What feeling is so nice as a child's
hand in yours? So small, so soft
and warm, like a kitten huddling
in the shelter of your clasp.*
—Marjorie Holmes

Love is harmony with others.

_____

*To be loved is to know happiness
and contentment.*
—Hardin Marshall

Break out of the everyday and
experience the joy of living.

_____

The less of routine, the more of life.
—Amos B. Alcott

You may find happiness in love, but
you will always learn by loving.

—————

A loving heart is the truest wisdom.
—Charles Dickens

Ask a riddle, tell a joke, or recite a
funny poem for the silliness of it.

———————

Mingle a little folly with your wisdom;
a little nonsense now and
then is pleasant.
—Carmina Horace

May your arms be as open
as your heart.

_____

*Love without ceasing, give
without measure.*
—Malcolm Schloss

Smile at a stranger today.

———————

*It's the little things we do and say that
mean so much as we go on our way.*
—Willa Hoey

Reach for the stars no matter
how far they are.

———————

Dream with your eyes open.
—Ernst Haas

Love and respect your family.
They love and respect you.

There is no friendship, no love like
that of the parent for the child.
  —Henry Ward Beecher

Life is built of experiences.
Remember the best ones.

––––––––––

*Childhood smells of perfume
and brownies.*
—David Leavitt

Be generous with your loved ones—
they will be generous with you.

————————

Happy homes are built of
blocks of patience.
—Harold E. Kohn

Give an acquaintance your love
and trust and you will receive
a friend in return.

———————

Friends share all things.
–Diogenes Laertius

Look within to find all that you need.

———————

Because of deep love, one is courageous.
—Lao Tzu

It is the simplicities in nature that are
the most soothing to your soul.

————————

'Tis the gift to be simple.
—"Shaker Gifts," Shaker hymn

The best defense is a smile.

———————————

Be happy. It's one way of being wise.
—Colette

Each morning, welcome
the start of a whole new world.

———

Today a new sun rises for me;
everything lives, everything is
animated, everything seems to
speak to me of my passion,
everything invites me to cherish it…
—Anne De Lenclos

Being alone, you will hurt no one, but
you will contribute nothing to humanity,
either. Be a part of life and experience
the power of give and take.

——————

*Nothing liberates our greatness like the
desire to help, the desire to serve.*
—Marianne Williamson

Dream.

———————

My motto—sans limites.
—Isadora Duncan

Honesty can be power and
is always right.

_____

*Peace means loyalty to self...A loyalty
to one's self means never a gap
between thought, speech, act.*
—Ruth Beebe Hill

You must desire change
to achieve progress.

———————————

*You are the architect of your
personal experience.*
–Shirley MacLaine

Love yourself as you love all the
beautiful creations around you,
because that is what you are!

---

*Truth exists for the wise, beauty for the
feeling heart.*
—Johann von Schiller

The ocean is always ready to give you a good lesson on the endless cycle of life and the eternal beauty of nature.

———————

Come my friends, 'tis not too late to seek a newer world, for my purpose holds to sail beyond the sunset.
—Alfred, Lord Tennyson, *Ulysses*

Celebrate the miracle of the
moment that you live in.

———————

*I love my past. I love my present.
I'm not ashamed of what I've had, and
I'm not sad because I have it no longer.*
—Colette

Treating each person with importance
is the easiest way to spread joy.

---

*How wonderful it is that nobody
need wait a single moment before
starting to improve the world.*
—Anne Frank

Let your heart be an open door that gives and receives love.

———————

My feeling is that there is nothing in life but refraining from hurting others, and comforting those that are sad.
—Olive Schreiner.

Even a difficult task is easy if your goal
is golden and your motives are pure.

_____

*The unendurable is the beginning
of the curve to joy.*
—Djuna Barnes

To work toward world peace, live it in your piece of the world.

———————

Love is not a doctrine. Peace is not an international agreement. Love and Peace are beings who live as possibilities.
—Mary Caroline Richards

Live in amazement of the
splendor of each day.

———————

This is what binds all people
and all creation together—the
gratuity of the gift of being.
—Matthew Fox

Spending the time to explore the overlooked details of a familiar place can be eye-opening and invigorating.

———————

*Nobody can conceive or imagine
all the wonders there are unseen
and unseeable in the world.*
—Francis P. Church

Each year, there are 365 (or 366) chances to seize a day and live it to the fullest. Go for a perfect record.

—————————

May you live all the days of your life.
—Jonathan Swift

A book is a vacation that you
don't have to pack for.

―――――――

*Reading is to the Mind, what
exercise is to the Body.*
―Joseph Addison

Choosing to love someone is the only gamble in life in which you win just by deciding to place a wager.

——————

To love is to place our happiness in the happiness of another.
—Gottfried Wilhelm von Leibniz

Sharing special memories with a friend lets you relive the past in order to strengthen the future.

———————

God gave us memory that we may have roses in December.
—James M. Barrie

To see an infant's smile is to experience
all that is good in the universe.

———————

A baby is God's opinion that
the world should go on.
—Carl Sandburg

Speak the truth to lift the spirit of others—but only when doing so will lift the spirit of others.

———————

Honesty is the first chapter in the book of wisdom.
—Thomas Jefferson

Dance, skip, and laugh with the joy of a child—freely and without care for what others may think.

—————

In every real man a child is hidden that wants to play.
—Friedrich Nietzsche

The only way to see the beauty
in all things is to believe that it is
there and then look for it.

—————

Beauty is not caused. It is.
—Emily Dickinson

Being spontaneous is fulfilling because
it forces you to be yourself.

———————

Life is short; eat dessert first.
—Joy Sommers

When you are truly listened to,
it makes you much more willing
to listen to someone else.

———————

*I cannot have what I want
if I don't wish it for others.*
—Betty MacDonald

Everyone is entitled to relax and enjoy
the life that has been given to them.

———————

Life is for enjoying. It is not a rat race
to see how much you can get done.
—Jill Clark

The world is a balancing act.
Even the darkest days are just
sunlight in disguise.

———————

Letting go of old hurts makes
room for new joys.
—Sefra Kobrin Pitzele

Once you believe that you belong on the team, you can start thinking about winning the game.

———————

Believe the best in yourself. Then it is easier to believe the best in others.
—Mardy Kopischke

There is a sparkly center of happiness in all of us; find it, treasure it, and let it shine.

—————————

A happy person is not a person in a certain set of circumstances, but rather a person with a certain set of attitudes.
—Hugh Downs

Few things are more thrilling than
seeing a shooting star.

———————

*Don't cry when the sun is gone, because
the tears won't let you see the stars.*
—Violeta Parra

Have a good old-fashioned snowball
fight in the front yard, then
come inside and share some
hot cocoa and memories.

———————

The best way to cheer yourself up is to
try to cheer somebody else up.
—Mark Twain

Glittering rays of sunshine are
free inspiration and all you have
to do is stand outside.

---

*Most of the shadows of this
life are caused by standing in
one's own sunshine.*
—Ralph Waldo Emerson

To aim high and believe in
your dreams is like taking
one step closer to pure joy.

———

*You can often measure a person
by the size of his dream.*
—Robert H. Schuller

Choose a life you are passionate
about and comfortable in.

———————

*Three grand essentials to happiness in
this life are something to do, something
to love, and something to hope for.*
—Joseph Addison

The greatest location in the whole universe is a place called home.

———————

From what we get, we can make a living; what we give, however, makes a life.
—Arthur Ashe

There is magic in sharing a fortune
cookie and finding it's written for two.

———————

*Let us be grateful to people who
make us happy; they are the charming
gardeners who make our souls blossom.*
—Marcel Proust

A hug should never be an arms-only
affair. Hug people with your whole self.
Get your heart involved. And let
the other person let go first.

———————

A hug is like a boomerang—
you get it back right away.
—Bill Keane

Moonlight sharpens in winter,
softens in summer,
and is beautiful year-round.

———————

Moonlight is sculpture.
–Nathaniel Hawthorne

Spring wouldn't be nearly as beautiful
if it didn't follow the long, dark
slumber of winter.

———————

*Let us learn to appreciate that there
will be times when the trees will be
bare, and look forward to the time
when we may pick the fruit.*
—Anton Chekhov

The most precious times in life are the
ones that surprise you and depart as
quickly as they showed up,
like shooting stars.

───────────

*Happiness is something that comes
into our lives through doors we don't
even remember leaving open.*
−Rose Wilder Lane

It's okay to be scared sometimes—
everyone is. Just remember that fear is
a very close cousin to exhilaration.

———————

Courage is the mastery of fear,
not the absence of fear.
—Mark Twain

In a world filled with noise and
confusion, we must train ourselves
to embrace those rare quiet moments
when we have the opportunity
to listen to our hearts.

———————

*There is always music amongst the
trees in the garden, but our hearts
must be very quiet to hear it.*
—Minnie Aumonier

Share stories. Tell jokes.
Really talk, and really listen.

———————

Among those whom I like or admire,
I can find no common denominator,
but among those whom I love, I can:
all of them make me laugh.
—W.H. Auden

Everyone has the potential to be
as wonder-struck and awe-filled
as a child because everyone was
a child once. The most important
instrument in inspiring wonder
in yourself is memory.

———————

*I still get wildly enthusiastic about little
things...I play with leaves. I skip down
the street and run against the wind.*
—Leo Buscaglia

When you are truly loved, you need never doubt it. Love never hides.

———————

Being deeply loved by someone gives you strength; loving someone deeply gives you courage.
—Lao Tzu

Rainy days are certainly dark
and gloomy. Yet they are responsible
for bringing forth all the beautiful
colors of spring. Love them for
the beauty they bring.

_____

*Keep your face to the sunshine and you
cannot see the shadow.*
—Helen Keller

A Book of Bliss

Your life is funnier than you think it is.
Look for the humor in the everyday
and you will find it.

———————

*If you're going to be able to look back
on something and laugh about it, you
might as well laugh about it now.*
—Marie Osmond

Have faith in life.
What is there otherwise?

————————

*When you come to the edge of all
that you know, you must believe one
of two things: There will be earth
upon which to stand, or you
will be given wings to fly.*
—unknown

Share the generosity you feel in your heart through good deeds and encouraging words.

———————

What I gave, I have; what I spent, I had; what I kept, I lost.
—old epitaph

What would you discover if you
remembered to ask, "What if?"

———————

*What if you slept? And what if, in
your sleep, you dreamed? And what if,
in your dream, you went to heaven
and there plucked a strange and
beautiful flower? And what if, when
you awoke, you had the flower in
your hand? Ah, what then?*
—Samuel Taylor Coleridge

Fairness brings the respect of other
and respect for oneself.

———————

Never elated when one man's oppress'd;
Never dejected while another's bless'd.
—Alexander Pope

Smiling makes everyone feel better.

———————

Those who bring sunshine to the lives of others cannot keep it from themselves.
—James Barrie

It is not necessary to acquire
to be rich in life.

———————

To live a pure, unselfish life,
one must count nothing as one's
own in the midst of abundance.
—Buddha

Don't think about what you may or may not be able to do. Live your life and the magic will appear.

———————

Aerodynamically, the bumble bee shouldn't be able to fly, but the bumble bee doesn't know it, so it goes on flying anyway.
—Mary Kay Ash

Embrace all the possibilities.

———————

*Go confidently in the direction
of your dreams. Live the life
you have imagined.*
—Henry David Thoreau

It's your life. Love it!

_____

Love is the river of life in the world
—Henry Ward Beecher

 A Book of Bliss

Be knowingly kind—
thoughtful generosity will lead
to automatic unselfishness.

———————

*We can be wise from goodness
and good from wisdom.*
–Marie von Ebner-Eschenback

Make something beautiful that
everyone can enjoy and you will have
brought grace to the world.

――――――

*Arranging a bowl of flowers in
the morning can give a sense of quiet
in a crowded day―like writing
a poem or saying a prayer.*
―Anne Morrow Lindbergh

If you remember to laugh, play,
and dance each day, youth
will always be yours.

———————

We are always the same age inside.
—Gertrude Stein

Awareness of life's gifts causes
them to touch us more deeply.

————————

*…I finally figured out the only reason
to be alive is to enjoy it.*
—Rita Mae Brown

Your talents not only give you the power to show what you are able to do, but also what you are willing to do.

———————

I can't write a book commensurate with Shakespeare, but I can write a book by me.
—Sir Walter Raleigh

Anything can be built from anything—a house from timber, a song from a passing word, love from grief.

———————

Do what you can, with what you have, where you are.
—Theodore Roosevelt

A Book of Bliss

If night never came,
we could never dream.

_____

When it gets dark enough,
you can see the stars.
—Lee Salk

Every day should be full of hugs!

———————

A hug is a perfect gift—one size fits all, and nobody minds if you exchange it.
—Ivern Ball

Let worries trouble you no more than
the wind through a wheat field.

––––––––––

*The turbulant billows of the fretful
surface leave the deep parts of the
ocean undisturbed.*
–William James

Choose to lead and others will follow.

————————

*I could tell where the lamplighter was
by the trail he left behind him.*
—Harry Lauder

If you learn to love and make friends with yourself, you will never be alone.

———————

When the friendly lights go out, there is a light by which the heart sees.
—Olga Rosmanith

A hammock and a lemonade bring
quiet peace to summer days.

———————

*Rest is not a matter of doing
absolutely nothing. Rest is repair.*
—Daniel W. Josselyn

Life is a journey. Don't look back.

———————

*I'm an idealist. I don't know where
I'm going but I'm on the way.*
—Carl Sandburg

What you need is within you.
Let the power of the world
compliment your own gifts.

———————

*It is not our circumstances that create
our discontent or contentment. It is us.*
—Vivian Greene

To join society one may do many things: work, vote, interact. To join with humanity one must love.

———————

There is only one happiness in life, to love and be loved.
—George Sand

They say talk is cheap. Show your loved ones that you care.

———————

Work is love made visible.
—Kahlil Gibran

A look, a touch,
a feeling can mean so very much.

———————

*Only love heals, makes whole, takes us
beyond ourselves. Love—not necessarily
mushy sentiment or docile passivity—is
both right motive and right result.*
—Marsha Sinetar

Share your wonder with others,
for it is through inspiration
that progress is made.

———————

It is up to you to illumine the Earth.
—Philippe Venier

Take your place in the world with
assuredness, because your existence
itself is justification for you.

———————

You are a child of the universe,
no less than the trees and the stars;
you have a right to be here.
—Desiderata

Experience and cherish the world.

———————

There are two ways to live your life.
One is as though nothing is a miracle.
The other is as though
everything is a miracle.
—Albert Einstein.

What delighted you as a child?
Remember the simple and fun things.

———————

The day is lost on which one has not laughed.
—French proverb

Enjoy the world around you.

----

*I am not afraid of tomorrow, for I have
seen yesterday and I love today.*
—William Allen White

 A Book of Bliss

A brave heart is a wise one.

———————

Nothing in life is to be feared.
It is only to be understood.
—Marie Curie

Friends and acquaintances can enrich our lives. Choose companions carefully so that you can benefit each other equally.

Walk with the wise and be wise; mix with the stupid and be misled.
—proverb

Give back to the world, for you benefit from it daily. Plant a tree or your favorite flowers.

Nature never did betray the heart that loved her.
—William Wordsworth

Hum, sing, or whistle
through your days.

———————

*Music produces a kind of pleasure that
human nature cannot do without.*
—Confucius

Exult in the magic of the morning,
the afternoon, the evening, and
the night. They are unique and
exactly as they should be.

_____

*Be intent upon the perfection
of the present day.*
–William Law

Rest renews us all: our minds,
our bodies, and our spirits.

———————

Tired nature's sweet restorer,
balmy sleep.
—Edward Young

A Book of Bliss

Celebrate nature and receive its glorious gifts.

I frequently tramped eight or ten miles through the deepest snow to keep an appointment with a beech tree or a yellow birch or an old acquaintance among the pines.
—Henry David Thoreau

Reap a rich future by
sowing plentifully now.

We write our own destiny.
We become what we do.
—Madame Chiang Kai-Shek

Children live in wonder because they seek. What could amaze you today?

———————

As I started looking,
I found more and more.
—Valerie Steele

You have all that you could need.

———————

The true exercise of freedom is—cannily and wisely and with grace—to move inside what space confines—and not seek to know what lies beyond and cannot be touched or tasted.
—A.S. Byatt

Sharing brings friends closer.

––––––––––

*Reinforce the stitch that ties us and I
will do the same for you.*
–Doris Schwerin

Being open to love and peace brings
more of both into the world.

───────────

*If you give your life as a wholehearted
response to love, then love will
wholeheartedly respond to you.*
—Marianne Williamson

There is a weightlessness to life
without regrets. Bear no grudges and
welcome others with a glad heart.

―――――――

*Forgiveness is the key to
action and freedom.*
―Hannah Arendt

Close your eyes and think of the most beautiful thing you can remember ever seeing. Now open your eyes and consider what surrounds you. It is all as beautiful as your memory.

. . .nothing is so humble that it cannot be made into art.
—Sari Dieves

Study, reading, and sharing
information keeps you young, vital,
and interested in the world.

————————

As we acquire more knowledge,
things to not become more
comprehensible, but more mysterious.
—Albert Schweitzer

The passions light the world, but
steadiness moves it.

———————

Talk gently; act frankly.
—William Henry Channing

Look forward to the rest of your life.
Goodness and lessons await.

———————

*Hope is itself a species of happiness
and, perhaps, the chief happiness
which this world affords.*
−Samuel Johnson

It takes character to give of yourself,
but the gift will be warmly received.

———————

What comes from the heart,
goes to the heart.
—Samuel Taylor Coleridge

The glories of the moment will inspire the hour; the victories of the morning will embolden the day; the triumphs of the present will shape the future.

————————

Light tomorrow with today!
—Elizabeth Barrett Browning.

Having a place to return to, where you
are loved, where you are comfortable,
where you love, is everything.

———————

*There is nothing like staying
at home for real comfort.*
—Jane Austen

Courage must come from a
passion to triumph and an
honest belief in one's rightness.

_____

The loving are the daring.
—Bayard Taylor

Travels show us the world,
but remind us where we belong.

———————

We only part to meet again.
—John Gay

We connect with ourselves,
others, and the universe
through music and song.

———————

Who hears music feels his
solitude peopled at once.
—Robert Browning

When in need of spiritual comfort,
go outside and let your
spirit soar with the clouds.

———————

The sky is the daily bread of the eyes.
–Ralph Waldo Emerson

Through words, through song,
through deeds: express yourself.

———————

Most joyful let the Poet be,
It is through him that all men see.
—William Ellery Channing

You could conquer the world,
but would have nothing unless
you had self-respect.

———————

The greatest success is successful
self-acceptance.
—Ben Sweet

No one else can be who you are,
so exercise your individuality.

———

Learn what you are, and be such.
—Pindar

Be positive and anything can happen.

———————

The world belongs to the
enthusiast who keeps cool.
—William McFee